# CAMPUS SPEECH IN CRISIS

# CAMPUS SPEECH IN CRISIS

*What the Yale Experience
Can Teach America*

*Introduction by* NATHANIEL A. G. ZELINSKY

*Commentary by* JOSÉ A. CABRANES
*and* KATE STITH

*With a preface by* GEORGE F. WILL

*A William F. Buckley, Jr. Program at Yale Book*

ENCOUNTER BOOKS
*New York · London*

# CONTENTS

# PREFACE

*George F. Will*

N EVER IN AMERICAN history has the freedom to speak been under such radical, comprehensive, and sustained attack.

Some opponents of free speech claim to merely want to "balance" the right to speak freely against other, supposedly competing, and often (they say) superior values. These include social harmony and individual serenity. But the freedom to speak has a way of disappearing by the time the balancing is completed.

Opponents of free speech often assert a new and countervailing right, the right to freedom from speech that they find distasteful, discomfiting, or inimical to the progress of History – this is, to them, a proper noun – toward its foreordained destination. People who think they know where History is headed do not think that free speech is needed in order to winnow truth from falsehood. Instead, censorship is needed to prevent misguided speech from delaying History's progressive unfolding.

Some of today's eager censors go beyond arguing that freedom to speak is a net subtraction from society's welfare. They add that free speech, a.k.a. "meaningful" free speech, is actually impossible. Incorporating into their arguments some familiar Marxist tropes about "false consciousness," such aspiring censors say: Because people do not really "make up their minds" – society does it for them – there is no particular urgency or dignity in allowing people to go around saying whatever they please.

The good news amid this welter of bad news is that individuals and institutions are joining the fray on behalf of the First Amendment and its assumptions. Readers of this pamphlet will appreciate the growing power of the gathering resistance to the new censorship. The censors are right about one thing: Speech is powerful. As they are about to find out, to their sorrow.

# INTRODUCTION TO
# THE WOODWARD REPORT

*Nathaniel A. G. Zelinsky*

THERE IS A CRISIS on American college campuses, a crisis of free expression.

By now, the pattern has become all too clear. First, a college extends an invitation to an outside guest, maybe to speak at a commencement or to deliver a lecture. Next, the protest begins. Students claim to be gravely offended – traumatized even – by the speaker's planned appearance and demand that the invitation be rescinded.

In some cases, weak-willed administrators acquiesce. The university issues a press release; it was a mistake to invite "so-and-so" to campus to receive an honor. In other cases, the guest does arrive, only to be met with turmoil and disruption. Either way, the planned address never happens.

Over the past few years, a number of American notables have fallen victim to campus censorship. Consider just a few:

In October 2013, protesters at Brown shouted down New York City's police commissioner, Ray Kelly, who could barely utter a word about the city's stop-and-frisk policy, the planned topic of his lecture.[1]

In April 2014, Brandeis disinvited Ayaan Hirsi Ali, to whom it had planned to award an honorary degree, after students and faculty took umbrage with her criticism of Islamic extremism.[2]

Later that fall, the president of Scripps College told George Will he was no longer welcome at Scripps because one of Will's opinion columns, regarding the issue of campus sexual assault, conflicted with the college's values.[3]

It isn't just outside speakers who suffer censorship on campus. Students come under attack just as often. When one Wesleyan undergraduate penned an article critical of the Black Lives Matter movement, the student government retaliated by slashing the budget of the newspaper that published the article.[4] Indicative of a trend to combat so-called "cultural appropriation," Bowdoin recently disciplined students who hosted and attended a fiesta-themed party where guests wore sombreros.[5]

To quote Yogi Berra, "It's déjà vu all over again."

In the 1960s and 1970s, college students across the United States adopted much of the same tactics and rhetoric that their modern peers employ. Go back fifty years, and you would see students similarly demanding disinvitations and disrupting events they found offensive.

At Yale University, a series of disturbing incidents in the 1970s led the school to form the Committee on Freedom of Expression, often called the Woodward Committee after its chairman, the eminent historian C. Van Woodward. First published in 1975 and reprinted in this booklet, the Woodward Committee's report vindicates honest debate, freedom of thought, and the open exchange of ideas. For modern defenders of free speech, the Woodward Report offers a timeless and timely explanation of why universities must protect the right of all to say all.

The history surrounding Yale's Woodward Report highlights the similarity between the past and present crises of free expression, with one important exception: the bar for censorship has fallen since the 1970s. Whereas yesterday's student protesters concerned themselves with issues of immense importance – from war to race relations – today's campus radicals seek to censor the most innocuous of transgressions, such as culturally appropriative sombreros.

❖ ❖ ❖

In the spring of 1974, a crowd of Yalies disrupted a debate that they deemed unacceptable. The topic to be debated: the sterilization of minorities.[6] On one side was the distinguished inventor of the transistor radio, William Shockley, who had become a late-in-life advocate for sterilization. His opponent, Bill Rusher, was the publisher of the conservative magazine *National Review*. (The sharp contrast between Shockley's outrageous beliefs and Commissioner Kelly's reasoned public policy preferences highlights how modern students will protest anything remotely controversial.)

The planned exchange never happened. Inside the lecture hall, an assembled crowd of two hundred and fifty students clapped, stomped, and chanted, preventing either man from saying a word. After an hour and fifteen minutes of raucous noise, Shockley and Rusher departed, and the protesters went home victorious.

The incident sparked a firestorm at Yale and in the national media. Shockley had previously spoken – with no incident – at Princeton, Columbia, and Amherst. While the university initially suspended twelve students for disrupting expression, the school later allowed them to return to campus.

For Yale's president, Kingman Brewster, the controversy was all too familiar. Free speech issues had dogged his tenure from the moment he had become acting president more than a decade before. In 1963, the Yale Political Union, a student group, invited Alabama's segregationist governor, George Wallace, to campus. That same semester, a bomb exploded in a black church in Birmingham, Alabama, killing four African-American children. Civil rights leaders blamed Wallace's political views for inspiring the bombing.

Convinced that hosting the governor at Yale

might inflame tensions among New Haven's African-American residents, Kingman Brewster met privately with students to urge them to rescind the invitation. New Haven's mayor, Richard Lee, declared Wallace "officially unwelcome in our community."[7] When the Political Union announced that it had retracted its offer, President Brewster publically thanked the students for their self-censorship.[8]

It seemed that Yale had caved to the threat of violence; pragmatic concerns outweighed free expression. The scandal deeply affected Brewster. In later years, debating difficult decisions, he would often tell himself to avoid the mistakes of the Wallace affair.[9]

As students mobilized against the Vietnam War – and for many other causes – disruptions became commonplace at colleges and universities. The paradigmatic protest involved a "sit-in," in which students occupied a building until administrators met their demands.

Yale survived without incident until 1969. When the university fired a dining hall worker, undergraduates condemned her abrupt dismissal and occupied her bosses' offices in a dingy basement. Forty-seven students refused to leave the office and administrators suspended them. Out of "mercy," the university committee responsible for discipline "commuted" the suspensions.[10] While not a traditional "free speech" incident in which protesters sought to censor others, the sit-in highlighted an important related question about the boundaries of free speech: should a university protect all actions, tactics, and words, including expression that seized public spaces for a private protest?[11]

Three years later, in April of 1972, Yale found itself at the center of yet another free speech crisis. General William Westmoreland, the former commander of U.S. forces in Vietnam, visited the campus to deliver an address. When a belligerent crowd gathered to protest his talk, the general refused to speak. A few days later, William P. Rogers, the secretary of state and former attorney general, canceled a trip to New Haven, after students threatened to censor his appearance. Once again, Yale seemed lawless and weak.

Finally, in 1975, the Shockley incident forced Yale's hand, and Kingman Brewster turned to a time-honored academic tradition for problem-solving: a student-faculty committee. From its inception, the committee's composition foretold its future product. Many of the faculty appointees were staunch defenders of free expression.

The committee's chairman, Professor C. Vann Woodward, was one of the greatest historians of his generation. A Southerner who was an outspoken opponent of segregation, Woodward had learned the values of tolerance, an ideal his fellow Southerners did not always extend to a man of his views. As a young academic, he protested McCarthysim during the 1950s; he saw in the left's censorship of the late 1960s the same authoritarian impulses that had driven the McCarthyites two decades earlier.[12] Woodward was impeccably liberal, a civil rights activist and a scholar who exposed what he famously termed the "Strange Career of Jim Crow" in a groundbreaking book of the same name in 1955.

Woodward's co-committee members were equally prestigious. One, Robert Dahl, was a prominent political scientist whose academic work defended liberal democracy against its critics.[13] Another, Harry Wellington, would become dean of the Yale Law School soon after the committee concluded its last meeting. Yalies could not easily dismiss a report by these men as the product of a stodgy conservative cabal.

The committee of thirteen faculty and students met during the fall term of 1974. The questions they discussed mirrored today's contemporary debate: Does everyone possess the right to speak? What are the boundaries of free speech? Is a sit-in or a disruptive protest itself a form of protected expression?

When it came time to write the report, dated 1974 but printed in 1975, the three prominent professors each spearheaded a section with assistance from the other committee members. To Dahl fell the first part of the report, which outlined the university's values. Woodward compiled a history of Yale's recent mishaps.[14] The third section – detailing the university's policies – fell to the lawyer, Wellington.[15] The edited portion of the report in this booklet contains much of Dahl's and Wellington's sections, though slightly less of Woodward's Yale-specific history.

Twelve of the thirteen committee members signed the final report. One student wrote a minority opinion that attacked the very notion of free expression. Although it quoted sixties philosophers who have fallen out of fad, the dissent echoes present-day arguments that "systemic inequality" and "class privilege" justify censorship.[16] Suppressing speech was defensible, this student wrote, when suppression liberated "the oppressed."

❖ ❖ ❖

The Woodward Report's lack of unanimity presaged free speech's troubled future over the next few decades. As the dissent highlighted, not everyone believed in the honest exchange of ideas. While Yale could boast of a strong affirmation of its values, the school would not always live up to the standards that Woodward, Dahl, and Wellington had set.

In the late 1980s, a Yale sophomore posted fliers mocking Gay and Lesbian Awareness Days – or GLAD – on campus. The fliers, comparing homosexuality to bestiality, were insensitive and offensive but clearly fell within the boundaries of protected discourse. Yet the university's executive committee found the student guilty of "harassment, intimidation, coercion, or assault."[17] Then-President A. Bartlett Giamatti declined to overturn the sentence. But when Giamatti departed Yale to lead baseball's National League, his successor, Benno Schmidt, a scholar of the First Amendment, invited the student to appeal the decision.[18] Still a member of the faculty, C. Vann Woodward successfully represented the offender – and the university committee reversed its verdict.[19]

More recently, free speech has again come under assault at Yale. In his first Freshman Address as Yale's twenty-third president in 2014, Peter Salovey celebrated the fortieth anniversary of the Woodward Report and reaffirmed its tenets as Yale's core principles.[20]

Only a year later, however, Yale found itself embroiled in a controversy once again. A female African-American student claimed that a fraternity denied her friends entry into a party because of a "white girls only" policy. (A subsequent university investigation could not substantiate her claims.)[21]

Around the same time, a faculty member and associate master of a residential college, Erika Christakis, emailed her students to criticize a memorandum, sent by a university committee, advocating that undergraduates wear culturally sensitive Halloween costumes:

*Is there no room anymore for a child or young person to be a little bit obnoxious ... a little bit inappropriate or provocative or, yes, offensive? American universities were once a safe space not only for maturation but also for a certain regressive, or even transgressive, experience; increasingly, it seems, they have become places of censure and prohibition.... If you don't like a costume someone is wearing, look away, or tell them you are offended. Talk to each other. Free speech and the ability to tolerate offence are the hallmarks of a free and open society.[22]*

The two events – a fraternity party and a relatively innocuous email – sparked massive protests. Students surrounded Nicholas Christakis, the master of the college[23] and Erika's husband, in the college's courtyard and berated him for his wife's words. Many called for the couple's resignation. The campus was a tinderbox, ready to explode.

At one point, alerted by a social media posting,

two hundred students sought to shut down a conference on free expression, fortuitously scheduled months beforehand. Only the well-timed response of the university's police prevented the mob from overrunning the conference hall.

Throughout the controversy, Peter Salovey and other administrators proclaimed that the Woodward Report was never in danger. In a subsequent call with alumni leaders and donors, Salovey highlighted the free speech conference as a shining exemplar of the open exchange of ideas – neglecting to mention that police were required to guard the conference against the disrupters. When events quieted down, Salovey later reaffirmed his commitment to a climate of tolerance and respect for views other than one's own.[24]

Future historians will debate why so many of today's students – at Yale and elsewhere – have vigorously embraced censorship. Regardless of the cause, an ideology has emerged couched in the language of "trigger warnings" and "safe spaces." According to this philosophy, offensive ideas do not just upset; they physically and mentally harm the listener. It was the "safe spaces" mantra that dominated the protests at Yale, and it is likely that this mantra will continue to plague campuses for the foreseeable future.

In reprinting the Woodward Report, this booklet hopes to once again refute the notion that speech should not be free. Other defenses of free expression exist, particularly a recent persuasive statement from the University of Chicago, which is included in an appendix to this booklet. However, the Woodward Report remains the premier document in the field. It should be required reading at all universities.

Also in this booklet are reflections on the Woodward Report by Judge José A. Cabranes and Professor Kate Stith. A United States Circuit Judge for the Second Circuit (which sits in New York), Judge Cabranes served as Yale's first general counsel and for many years as the trustee of a number of institutions of higher learning, including Yale. Professor Stith teaches at the Yale Law School as the Lafayette S. Foster Professor of Law and was previously a trustee of Dartmouth College, her alma mater.

In their reflections, Judge Cabranes and Professor Stith remember a time when Yale printed the Woodward Report in a booklet – not unlike this one – as a reminder of the school's commitment to free expression. If history is a guide, attacks on free speech will persist and many administrators will likely consent to censorship rather than stand for the values of open discourse. As they did in 1975, however, Woodward and his colleagues offer another path, one in which ideas, not intolerance, reign.

# CHAIRMAN'S LETTER
# TO THE FELLOWS OF
# THE YALE CORPORATION

*December 23, 1974*

To the Fellows of the Yale Corporation:[1]

THE FOLLOWING REPORT is the result of the findings and deliberations of a committee appointed last September by President Kingman Brewster, Jr. The President was responding in part to a resolution adopted by the Yale College Faculty on May 2, 1974, requesting him "to appoint a faculty commission to examine the condition of free expression, peaceful dissent, mutual respect and tolerance at Yale, to draft recommendations for any measures it may deem necessary for the maintenance of those principles, and to report to the faculties of the University early next term." Guided by the Rules of Governance adopted in 1970, the President appointed a committee of thirteen consisting of five faculty members, two members of the administration, three graduate students, two undergraduates, and one member of the Yale alumni. Their names, with one exception, will be found at the end of the report.

In efforts to fulfill its assignment the committee not only reviewed the record of the past decade but also sought to inform itself about attitudes and opinions of all members of the University community who wished to make their views known. Repeated invitations in the press brought in numerous written statements, many of them thoughtful and informative. The committee also held advertised public as well as private hearings and recorded hours of testimony and advice.

It is gratifying to report that the committee found strong support for the maintenance and defense of freedom of expression among those whose views were received. A smaller number held reservations of various kinds about how much freedom should be tolerated. Some felt that freedom of speech was too dangerous, or that enjoyment of free speech should await the establishment of equality or the liberation of the oppressed. Only one appeared willing to advocate censorship and suppression of unpopular speakers.

How well the views last mentioned are represented in the dissenting statement of one member of the committee it is impossible to say. At least it serves as some indication of the difficulties the University might face in implementing the principles supported by the committee. Printed exactly as delivered, the dissenting member's statement was only received after the committee had finished its deliberations, completed the writing of its report, and disbanded for the holidays. The committee was therefore unable to comment on the faithfulness with which its views are represented, the scrupulousness with which its words are quoted, or the accuracy of factual allegations.[2]

From the beginning of its investigations the committee has been aware that Yale's problems are shared by sister institutions at home and abroad. Correspondence with some of them has reinforced the impression that a movement which in its inception in California a decade ago proudly invoked the name of Free Speech has in latter days showed signs of repudiating its original commitment. While this investigation is confined to the experience at Yale, it has been the hope of the committee that its statement might inspire in other universities a rededication to the principles asserted in this report.

❖ ❖ ❖

C. Vann Woodward
*Chairman*

# THE REPORT OF
# THE COMMITTEE

## I. OF VALUES AND PRIORITIES

*And though all the winds of doctrine were let loose to play upon the earth, so Truth be in the field, we do injuriously by licensing and prohibiting to misdoubt her strength. Let her and Falsehood grapple; who ever knew Truth put to the worse, in a free and open encounter.*

JOHN MILTON
*Areopagitica*, 1644

*If there is any principle of the Constitution that more imperatively calls for attachment than any other it is the principle of free thought – not free thought for those who agree with us but freedom for the thought that we hate.*

OLIVER WENDELL HOLMES, JR.
*U.S. v. Schwimmer*, 1928

THE PRIMARY FUNCTION of a university is to discover and disseminate knowledge by means of research and teaching. To fulfill this function a free interchange of ideas is necessary not only within its walls but with the world beyond as well. It follows that the university must do everything possible to ensure within it the fullest degree of intellectual freedom. The history of intellectual growth and discovery clearly demonstrates the need for unfettered freedom, the right to think the unthinkable, discuss the unmentionable, and challenge the unchallengeable. To curtail free expression strikes twice at intellectual freedom, for whoever deprives another of the right to state unpopular views necessarily also deprives others of the right to listen to those views.

We take a chance, as the First Amendment takes a chance, when we commit ourselves to the idea that the results of free expression are to the general benefit in the long run, however unpleasant they may appear at the time. The validity of such a belief cannot be demonstrated conclusively. It is a belief of recent historical development, even within universities, one embodied in American constitutional doctrine but not widely shared outside the academic world, and denied in theory and in practice by much of the world most of the time.

Because few other institutions in our society have the same central function, few assign such high priority to freedom of expression. Few are expected to. Because no other kind of institution combines the discovery and dissemination of basic knowledge with teaching, none confronts quite the same problems as a university.

For if a university is a place for knowledge, it is also a special kind of small society. Yet it is not primarily a fellowship, a club, a circle of friends, a replica of the civil society outside it. Without sacrificing its central purpose, it cannot make its primary and dominant value the fostering of friendship, solidarity, harmony, civility, or mutual respect. To be sure, these are important values; other institutions may properly assign them the highest, and not merely a subordinate priority; and a good university will seek and may in some significant measure attain these ends. But it will never let these values, important as they are, override its central purpose. We value freedom of expression precisely because it provides a forum for the new, the provocative, the disturbing, and the unorthodox. Free speech is a barrier to the tyranny of authoritarian or even majority opinion as to the rightness or wrongness of particular doctrines or thoughts.

If the priority assigned to free expression by the nature of a university is to be maintained in practice, clearly the responsibility for maintaining that priority rests with its members. By voluntarily taking up membership in a university and thereby asserting a claim to its rights and privileges, members also acknowledge the existence of certain obligations upon themselves and their fellows. Above all, every member of the university has an obligation to permit free expression in the university. No member has a right to prevent such expression. Every official of the university, moreover, has a special obligation to foster free expression and to ensure that it is not obstructed.

The strength of these obligations, and the willingness to respect and comply with them, probably depend less on the expectation of punishment for violation than they do on the presence of a widely shared belief in the primacy of free expression. Nonetheless, we believe that the positive obligation to protect and respect free expression shared by all members of the university should be enforced by appropriate formal sanctions, because obstruction of such expression threatens the central function of the university. We further believe that such sanctions should be made explicit, so that potential violators will be aware of the consequences of their intended acts.

In addition to the university's primary obligation to protect free expression there are also ethical responsibilities assumed by each member of the university community, along with the right to enjoy free expression. Though these are much more difficult to state clearly, they are of great importance. If freedom of expression is to serve its purpose, and thus the purpose of the university, it should seek to enhance understanding. Shock, hurt, and anger are not consequences to be weighed lightly. No member of the community with a decent respect for others should use, or encourage others to use, slurs and epithets intended to discredit another's race, ethnic group, religion, or sex. It may sometimes be necessary in a university for civility and mutual respect to be superseded by the need to guarantee free expression. The values superseded are nevertheless important, and every member of the university community should consider them in exercising the fundamental right to free expression.

We have considered the opposing argument that behavior which violates these social and ethical considerations should be made subject to formal sanctions, and the argument that such behavior entitles others to prevent speech they might regard as offensive. Our conviction that the central purpose of the university is to foster the free access of knowledge compels us to reject both of these arguments. They assert a right to prevent free expression. They rest upon the assumption that speech can be suppressed by anyone who deems it false or offensive. They deny what Justice Holmes termed "freedom for the thought that we hate." They make the majority, or any willful minority, the arbiters of truth for all. If expression may be prevented, censored or punished, because of its content or because of the motives attributed to those who promote it, then it is no longer free.

It will be subordinated to other values that we believe to be of lower priority in a university.

The conclusions we draw, then, are these: even when some members of the university community fail to meet their social and ethical responsibilities, the paramount obligation of the university is to protect their right to free expression. This obligation can and should be enforced by appropriate formal sanctions. If the university's overriding commitment to free expression is to be sustained, secondary social and ethical responsibilities must be left to the informal processes of suasion, example, and argument.

## II. OF TRIALS AND ERRORS

Part of the Committee's charge was to assess the condition of freedom of expression at Yale. This requires some search of the University's record, good, bad, and indifferent, in defending its principles. The full history is too long and complicated to unfold here, but there are more reasons for concentrating on the recent past than lack of space and time. It is not clear, for one thing, how early in its history Yale's commitment to these principles became firm. Nor is it clear how much is to be gained by comparing in this respect the old Yale with the new Yale of recent years.

While the old Yale laid valid claim to being a national institution with representatives in its student body and faculty from all parts of the country and many parts of the world, in significant ways it was more homogeneous than the new Yale. One consequence of that homogeneity was the absence of some divisions that would plague the future. Changes in policies of recruitment, admission, and grants of assistance replaced the relative homogeneity of old Yale with the heterogeneity of new Yale. The decade of the sixties brought larger delegations of classes, races, and ethnic groups that had been underrepresented before or not present at all. The new groups were more self-conscious as minorities and others were more conscious of them. Reactions ranged from insensitivity for minority points of view to paternalistic solicitude for minority welfare and feelings. And sometimes insensitivity and solicitude commingled.

The new heterogeneity did not prevent the forging of a strongly held consensus on certain issues. One of them was civil rights, and especially the rights of black people. Another was opposition to the Vietnam War and a multitude of policies associated with it. Yale shared in full the spirit of political activism and radical protest that swept the major campuses in the sixties. Storms of controversy and crises of confrontation broke over the campus with a force comparable to that which crippled some of the country's strongest universities. Yale was generally regarded as exceptionally fortunate in its ability to weather the years of crisis. Some thought the University led a charmed life, and while President Brewster had numerous critics, others attributed Yale's comparative stability to the quality of leadership provided by his administration. A complete account of those years, even a full study of free speech during the sixties would contain much in which Yale could take pride. Placed in the context of failures elsewhere, the failures at home – and they are serious enough to cause concern – would loom less large.

The University's commitment to the principle of freedom of expression was put to severe tests during the years of campus upheaval. It should be noted, however, that the main incidents of equivocation and failure with which this report is concerned did not coincide with the years of storm and stress. The first incident, that of the invitation to Governor George C. Wallace, occurred in 1963, before the full onset of the critical period. The others came in 1972, after the tumult had subsided, and in 1974, a year of relative tranquillity. The latter incidents are those involving General William Westmoreland, Secretary of State William Rogers, and Professor William Shockley. Only the last of them culminated in actions that physically prevented a speaker from being heard when he appeared before an audience. The other scheduled speakers did not actually appear before an audience for various reasons, including the withdrawal of an invitation, decisions by invitees not to appear, and threats of disruption and possible violence. But failure or equivocation in defense of free speech was fairly attributable to the University community in some degree in at least three and possibly all four incidents.

It should be recalled that the record of the University includes successes as well as failures, and that the successes in defense of principle were not all on the side of speakers who supported the University consensus on the war and racial issues. In spite of prevailing hostility to their views on the part of a large campus majority, General Curtis LeMay, Governor Ronald Reagan, Senator Barry Goldwater, and Professor Richard Herrnstein[3] were invited, received, and heard during these years.

The first of the failures came in the fall of 1963 when the Political Union invited Governor George C. Wallace of Alabama to speak at Yale.

❖ ❖ ❖

This committee's account has revealed instances of faltering, uncertainty, and failure in the defense of principle on the part of various elements in the University community. Within the community has appeared from time to time a willingness to compromise standards, to give priority to peace and order and amicable relations over the principle of free speech when it threatens these other values. Elements within the University community have shown since the time of the Wallace incident signs of declining commitment to the defense of freedom of expression in the University.

A significant number of students and some faculty members appear to believe that when speakers are offensive to majority opinion, especially on such issues as war and race, it is permissible and even desirable to disrupt them; that there is small chance of being caught, particularly among a mass of offenders; that if caught there is a relatively good chance of not being found guilty; and that if found guilty no serious punishment is to be expected. In the only instance of massive infraction of free speech in which offenders were subject to disciplinary action, that of the Shockley case, experience lent support to some of these assumptions.

From the administration have come promptings that have at times been mixed and contradictory. It is true that in each of the crises reviewed and in many other critical situations during the troubled decade just ended President Brewster has voiced the University's commitment to freedom of expression, "to untrammelled individual initiative in preference to conformity," and to academic freedom generally. It is also true that the administration has never barred outright an invitation to speak; it has assigned halls on request, and has warned against disruption. In specific instances, however, statements by the President and the Corporation have been interpreted as assigning equal if not higher value to law and order, to town-gown relations, to proper motives, to the sensitivity of those who feel threatened or offended, and to majority attitudes. Some of the statements have placed blame for failure not only on the disrupters and their lawlessness, but also upon the inviters of the speakers and their motives, and on the views of the proposed speakers as well. Moreover, the University's physical arrangements for deterring and detecting disrupters have proved inadequate. And finally, the faculty has not been as alert as it might have been to these problems.

This committee, therefore, finds a need for Yale to reaffirm a commitment to the principle of freedom of expression and its superior importance to other laudable principles and values, to the duty of all members of the University community to defend the right to speak and refrain from disruptive interference, and to the sanctions that should be imposed upon those who offend.

We agree with President Brewster's statement in his baccalaureate address of 1974, that "the prospects and processes of punishment" and the "lust for retribution" constitute no adequate solution – though we would urge clearer definition and more vigorous enforcement of rules. Rules and their enforcement must rest upon a consensus of the whole community on the principle of freedom of expression and a genuine concern over violations. To build this consensus we make the suggestions set forth in Part III of this report.

## III. OF WAYS AND MEANS

The foregoing review has persuaded this committee that the time has come to revitalize our principles, to reaffirm and renew our commitment, and to find ways and means for the effective and vigorous defense of our values. To promote these ends we propose:

First, that a program of reeducation is required. Some members of the university do not fully appreciate the value of the principle of freedom of expression. Nor is this surprising. In one of his most famous dissents, Mr. Justice Holmes spoke to the question:

> *Persecution for the expression of opinions seems to me perfectly logical. If you have no doubt of your premises or your power and want a certain result with all your heart you naturally express your wishes in law and sweep away all opposition. To allow opposition by speech seems to indicate that you think the speech impotent, as when a man says that he has squared the circle, or that you do not care wholeheartedly for the result, or that you doubt either your power or your premises. But when men have realized that time has upset many fighting faiths, they may come to believe even more than they believe the very foundations of their own conduct that the ultimate good desired is better reached by free trade in ideas...*
>
> *Abrams v. U.S.,* 1919

Education in the value of free expression at Yale is the business of all sectors of the University.

Much needs to be done. The first need is for effective and continuing publication of the University's commitment to freedom of expression. At present, only two readily available documents address the subject and suggest standards of conduct: the Yale College "Undergraduate Regulations" and the "Rights and Duties of Members of the Yale Law School." We urge that all University catalogues, as well as the faculty and staff handbooks, include explicit statements on freedom of expression and the right to dissent. And that the attention of students should be directed to these statements each year at registration. We also urge that each school – its dean, its faculty, and its students – consider the most effective ways to clarify and discuss the relation of free expression to the mission of the University. These might include addresses to entering students, discussions in informal settings such as the residential colleges, and special attention to the subject in student publications.

Second, that individuals and groups who object to a controversial speaker should understand the limits of protest in a community committed to the principles of free speech. Let us therefore be clear about those limits.

1. It is desirable that individuals and groups register in a wide-open and robust fashion their opposition to the views of a speaker with whom they disagree or whom they find offensive. When such a speaker has been invited to the campus by one group, other groups may seek to dissuade the inviters from proceeding. But it is a punishable offense against the principles of the University for the objectors to coerce others physically or to threaten violence.

2. The permissible registration of opposition includes all forms of peaceful speech, such as letters to newspaper editors, peaceful assembly, and counter-speeches in appropriate locations. Furthermore, picketing is permissible outside of a building so long as it is peaceful and does not interfere with entrance to or exit from the building or with pedestrian or vehicular traffic outside of a building. It is important to understand, however, that picketing is

more than expression. It is expression joined to action. Accordingly, it is entitled to no protection when its effect is coercive.

3. There is no right to protest within a university building in such a way that any university activity is disrupted. The administration, however, may wish to permit some symbolic dissent within a building but outside the meeting room, for example, a single picket or a distributor of handbills.

4. In the room where the invited speaker is to talk, all members of the audience are under an obligation to comply with a general standard of civility. This means that any registration of dissent that materially interferes with the speaker's right to proceed is a punishable offense. Of course a member of the audience may protest in a silent, symbolic fashion, for example, by wearing a black arm band. More active forms of protest may be tolerated such as briefly booing, clapping hands, or heckling. But any disruptive activity must stop when the chair or an appropriate university official requests silence.

Failure to quit in response to a reasonable request for order is a punishable offense.

5. Nor does the content of the speech, even parts deemed defamatory or insulting, entitle any member of the audience to engage in disruption. While untruthful and defamatory speech may give rise to civil liability it is neither a justification nor an excuse for disruption, and it may not be considered in any subsequent proceeding against offenders as a mitigating factor. Nor are racial insults or other "fighting words" a valid ground for disruption or physical attack – certainly not from a voluntary audience invited but in no way compelled to be present. Only if speech advocates immediate and serious illegal action, such as burning down a library, and there is danger that the audience will proceed to follow such an exhortation, may it be stopped, and then only by an authorized university official or law enforcement officer.

6. The banning or obstruction of lawful speech can never be justified on such grounds as that

the speech or the speaker is deemed irresponsible, offensive, unscholarly, or untrue.

Third, the University could be more effective in discharging its obligation to use all reasonable effort to protect free expression on campus. We submit that this obligation can be discharged most effectively in the following ways:

1. The University and its schools should retain an open and flexible system of registering campus groups, arranging for the reservation of rooms, and permitting groups freely to invite speakers.

2. It is entirely appropriate, however, for the President and other members of the administration to attempt to persuade a group not to invite a speaker who may cause serious tension on campus. This is best done by communicating directly with the inviting group. It is appropriate for the University official to explain to the group its moral obligations to other members of the community. It is important, however, for the official to make it

clear that these are moral obligations for the inviters to weigh along with other considerations in deciding whether to go forward, and that a decision to go forward is one which carries no legal or disciplinary consequences nor risks of more subtle University reprisals.

3. Once an invitation is accepted and the event is publicly announced, there are high risks involved if a University official – especially the President – attempts by public or private persuasion to have the invitation rescinded. There is a risk that the public or private attempt will appear as an effort to suppress free speech, and also a risk that a public attempt will lend "legitimacy" to obstructive action by those who take offense at the speaker. Should the President or any other University official think it necessary to make such an attempt, however, it is important that he also make it plain that if his appeal is disregarded, (a) no disciplinary jeopardy will attach to the inviting group, and (b) the University will make every effort to insure that the speech takes place.

4. Generally the inviting group should be free to decide whether the speech will be open to the public. However, if the administration has reasonable cause to believe that outsiders will be disruptive, it may appropriately limit attendance to members of the University. The duty of the administration is to uphold free speech within the university community and to insure that a speaker be heard. To discharge this duty it must have the power to impose sanctions against disrupters. It has little power against outside offenders against its rules.

5. The administration's obligation to protect freedom of expression also means that when it has reasonable cause to anticipate disruption, it may require that individuals produce University I. D. cards to gain admission. We suggest that such cards be issued to all members of the University and that they include a photograph.

6. Much can be done to forestall disruption if sufficient notice is given of the impending event. The administration and others can meet with protesting groups, make clear the

University's obligations to free expression, and indicate forms of dissent that do not interfere with the right to listen. The inviting group can work closely with the administration to devise the time, place, and arrangements for admitting the audience (if there are any limits on who may attend) that will best promote order.

7. When the administration has reasonable cause to anticipate disruption, it should designate a particular hall as one best suited to protect a speaker from disruption and make that hall as secure as is reasonably possible. Effective arrangements for identifying offenders such as the use of cameras can serve as a deterrant [*sic*].

8. A group inviting a speaker may close the meeting to the press. It also may invite the press. In either case, the administration should cooperate.

If a group wishes to arrange for television coverage, it should discuss the matter with an appropriate University official. Television should be permitted if the inviting group desires, unless the President or a person designated by him determines that the presence of television will itself make it substantially more likely that serious disruption will occur. If such a determination is made, it is the obligation of the administration to forbid television and to declare that the presence of television increases the risk of thwarting free expression and puts individuals and the property of the University at high risk.

9. The administration's responsibility for assuring free expression imposes further obligations: it must act firmly when a speech is disrupted or when disruption is attempted; it must undertake to identify disrupters, and it must make known its intentions to do so beforehand.

These obligations can be discharged in two ways. One, the administration may call the city police and the criminal law. This is undesirable except where deemed absolutely necessary to protect individuals and property, for police presence can itself lead to injury and violence. Two, the administration can make clear in advance that serious sanctions will be imposed upon those who transgress the limits of legitimate protest and engage in disruption. It is plain, however, that if sanctions are to work as a deterrent to subsequent disruption, they must be imposed whenever disruption occurs. They must be imposed and not suspended. They must stick.

10. Disruption of a speech is a very serious offense against the entire University and may appropriately result in suspension or expulsion. Accordingly, one who is alleged to have committed such an offense should be tried before the University-Wide Tribunal. The Tribunal's jurisdiction should vest upon complaint by the President or Provost. The collective assent of the deans should not be required in cases of this sort.

We believe that the procedures established in the charter of the University-Wide Tribunal and the sanctions that the Tribunal may impose are well suited to so serious an offense as the disruption of free expression.

Steven A. Benner
*Yale College, 1975*

Elias Clark
*Master of Silliman College,*
*Lafayette S. Foster Professor of Law*

James P. Comer
*Associate Professor of Psychiatry,*
*Associate Dean of the Medical*
*School*

Lloyd N. Cutler
*Visiting Lecturer in Law,*
*Chairman Yale Development*
*Board*

Robert A. Dahl
*Sterling Professor of Political*
*Science*

Marjorie B. Garber
*Associate Professor of English*

Walter R. Rieman
*Yale College, 1977*

Philip J. Sirlin
*Princeton, 1973, Graduate Student*
*in Economics*

Elisabeth McC. Thomas
*Dean Pierson College,*
*Assistant Dean of Yale College*

Hillel Weinberg
*State University of N.Y., Buffalo,*
*1973, Graduate Student in*
*Political Science*

Harry H. Wellington
*Edward J. Phelps Professor of Law*

C. Vann Woodward
*Sterling Professor of History*
*(Chairman)*

# FREE SPEECH IN OUR UNIVERSITIES
A Commentary on the Woodward Report[1]

*José A. Cabranes and Kate Stith*

THE WOODWARD COMMITTEE'S January 8, 1975 report was a milestone in the history of free expression in higher education. At Yale, it was accorded something akin to constitutional status, printed by the Yale Corporation in the same format and handsome binding used for the university's charter and by-laws. The Woodward Report has been memorialized in various Yale policies,[2] and its recommended procedures for dealing with unanticipated disruptions of campus life have frequently served as a kind of handbook for administrators "on those periodic occasions when some very public campus event has required a reminder of why free speech is so important."[3]

Woodward and his colleagues accorded free expression on a private university campus a degree of protection close to that afforded by the First

Amendment in the public sphere. Indeed, the Woodward Report begins by quoting Justice Oliver Wendell Holmes, Jr.'s famous dissent in *United States v. Schwimmer*: "[I]f there is any principle of the Constitution that more imperatively calls for attachment than any other it is the principle of free thought – not free thought for those who agree with us but freedom for the thought that we hate."[4]

That this principle of constitutional law should also be a principle of university administration is explained by a simple syllogism. "The primary function of a university is to discover and disseminate knowledge." "To fulfill this function a free interchange of ideas is necessary." Therefore, "the university must do everything possible to ensure within it the fullest degree of intellectual freedom."

Because "the paramount obligation of the university is to protect [the] right to free expression," values other than free speech are "of lower priority in a university." The Woodward Report's free speech values, like those of the First Amendment, are expansive, encompassing "unfettered freedom, the right to think the unthinkable, discuss the unmentionable, and challenge the unchallengeable."

The Woodward Report proposes three "ways and means for the effective and vigorous defense of our values." First, the university should educate its members about free speech values, both formally and informally. Second, the university should clarify "the limits of protest in a community committed to the principles of free speech." Yale's robust commitment to free expression forecloses not only violence against disfavored speakers, but also certain other forms of obstruction, such as the occupation of buildings, which have a fundamentally coercive effect. Third, the university should outline appropriate steps to take when a group invites a controversial speaker.

The Woodward Report notes countervailing forces that might present persistent challenges to a community in which free expression is accorded the highest value. The right to free speech on campus competes with other values, including "the fostering of friendship, solidarity, harmony, civility or mutual respect," egalitarianism, town-gown relations, sensitivity to offending racial and other minorities, and the security of controversial speakers. Subsequent events add to this list sensitivity to sexual minorities, rights to privacy, the elimination of hostility to women, and the security of members of the university. The report recognized these goals as important, and it urged members of the Yale community to "consider them in exercising the fundamental right to free expression." Ultimately, however, the balancing of these competing values was an "ethical responsibilit[y] assumed by each member of the university community," rather than a task for the university itself, which retained the "primary" and "overriding" obligation to protect free expression.

Importantly, the Woodward Report rejects the limited interpretation of free speech favored by some timid or eager-to-please administrators. Approaching the problem of terminology, the report addresses *intellectual* freedom – the freedom that protects speech and expression on campus, particularly obnoxious speech, and not only the speech of the mandarin class of tenured professors. *Academic* freedom, by contrast, is the prescriptive right of tenured faculty to teach and research what they choose without outside influence. Intellectual freedom is broader than academic freedom. In particular, *intellectual* freedom protects speech and expression, including obnoxious speech, of *all* on campus. It shelters the student lounge no less than the faculty lounge.

Since the mid-1970s, a variety of social and political forces have challenged the commitment of Yale and other universities to the freedom of expression. Two developments are particularly worthy of mention. First, some governmental agencies have developed broad concepts of "harassment" that encompass hitherto protected speech. In particular, the Department of Education's Office for Civil Rights (OCR) and the U.S. Department of Justice have pressured universities to punish, as "sexual harassment," "*any* unwelcome conduct of a sexual nature" – whether or not that conduct would be objectively offensive to a reasonable person.[5] In the words of Nadine Strossen, the former longtime president of the American Civil Liberties Union, this standard effectively forbids "any expression with any sexual content that anyone subjectively finds offensive no matter how unreasonably or irrationally."[6] Under this aggressive redefinition of antidiscrimination law,[7] universities face significant pressure – real or perceived – to discipline students and faculty members for speech in print, in the classroom, or elsewhere on or off campus that runs afoul of a particular agency's gender orthodoxy.[8]

Second, universities, including Yale, have declared a commitment to "civility"; in Yale's case, this includes a decree that students at Yale College shall "value civility in all their interactions and [ ] maintain a sensitivity to the circumstances and feelings that inform their ideas." The result is curious indeed: those who are part of the university community may have less freedom of speech than those from outside the university who are invited on an *ad hoc* basis to speak on campus.

The threat to free expression has emerged especially from the declarations of some groups of students – in the undisputed exercise of their own speech rights – that they have been victims of uncivil, disrespectful, or simply hateful speech. In some cases, these groups also proclaim themselves victims of a "hostile" or offensive "environment" created by insensitive students and others who must therefore be punished. In the face of such declarations, the defense of free expression necessarily falls on the shoulders of administrators, some tenured but most not, who themselves may feel beleaguered by the offended groups, but who are nevertheless intent on avoiding offense.

In these contests between wounded, sensitive victims and "uncivil" or hateful offenders, freedom of speech is on the line, just as Woodward and his colleagues predicted. The offended may purport to speak for large numbers, often through megaphones provided by national constituencies, while the putative offenders find themselves suddenly vulnerable because their disfavored speech runs afoul of a mobilized public opinion. Under stress, administrators clutch the talisman of "community" and soon tend to morph into campus monitors of acceptable speech – and, ultimately, into the unhappy role of Civility Police. In these cases, administrators at universities like Yale cannot feel good or look good. Hounded by officious regulatory agencies, and fearful of more harmful publicity, they submit to prolonged internal or external investigations. Although these investigations are allegedly "confidential," the complaining parties freely feed information and misinformation to a hungry media, on and off campus, to project their grievances to the nation.

These dramas end, almost inevitably, with the university confessing to some vaguely described errors or inadequacies. The investigating organization – whether OCR, another governmental agency, or a unit of the university itself – will announce that it has completed its "investigation" and has reached an "agreement" with the university or a particular department thereof. ("Agreement" is an especially important word when governmental agencies are involved: OCR seldom litigates serious matters, and its "voluntary" resolutions with universities are not subject to judicial review.) The university artfully avoids any suggestion of legal liability but nevertheless effectively confesses guilt and agrees to perform various acts of penance. Its self-punishment may take many forms: public criticism by administrators of "uncivil" speech and speakers; punishing of organizations associated with, or individuals who engaged in, offensive speech; and punitive action against organizations with no history of offensive behavior other than their mere existence as all-male voluntary associations.[9] Universities may also agree to adopt yet another set of "procedures" – often "recommended" by OCR, and thus effectively required by the federal government – meant to handle future grievances of this sort.[10]

Although the details vary, each of these campus dramas ultimately conflates offensive speech with truly dangerous behavior. Sexual assault, sexually charged threats, and sex-related comments – whether personal, political, or pedagogical – all fall under the broad rubric of "sexual misconduct."[11] Campuses can be rendered "unsafe" not only by actual threats against particular minority groups, but by controversial messages.[12] As a result, university "Civility Police" have started to adopt the tactics of the real police – but to fight speech, not crime. For instance, university "Bias Response Teams" investigate not only actual crimes, such as vandalism or assault, but also professors' online comments and the editorial choices of the campus press.[13] Even more troublingly, some universities are exploring *anonymous* reporting mechanisms, which enable users to report offensive comments to university administrators online or through a smartphone app.[14]

Anonymous tips can be an important tool, albeit a controversial one, for catching criminals and others who pose a serious threat to the physical safety of others.[15] But our legal system long recognized that anonymous tips carry a heightened risk of abuse. That is true even with respect to 911 calls, which are recorded, and which therefore provide victims of false reports an opportunity to identify and to prosecute the false tipster.[16] Such protections are conspicuously absent, however, from the proposals of those who suggest that college students and other members of the university community require a system of secret surveillance in order to be protected from obnoxious speech.[17]

None of this is to say that university administrators must stand idly by while students face threats, harassment, or discrimination. The Woodward Report itself allows administrators to voice "other values," as long as they do not censor speech. And, of course, universities – like the government – have the right, and sometimes the duty, to protect students from physical violence and to offer them the medical, emotional, and spiritual support necessary to navigate the conflict and discomfort that often accompany vigorous debate. But when administrators condemn offensive speech or offensive speakers, they blur the lines between endorsing "other values," educating the community, and viewpoint censorship.

The principles of free expression pronounced and codified in the Woodward Report will always be at risk when the values of "civility" and "community" compete for primacy in the hearts and minds of those the report charges with the "effective and vigorous defense" of the right to free expression on campus.[18]

# APPENDIX
Report of the Committee
on Freedom of Expression,
University of Chicago

*The Committee on Freedom of Expression at the University of Chicago was appointed in July 2014 by President Robert J. Zimmer and Provost Eric D. Isaacs "in light of recent events nationwide that have tested institutional commitments to free and open discourse." The Committee's charge was to draft a statement "articulating the University's overarching commitment to free, robust, and uninhibited debate and deliberation among all members of the University's community."*

*The Committee has carefully reviewed the University's history, examined events at other institutions, and consulted a broad range of individuals both inside and outside the University. This statement reflects the long-standing and distinctive values of the University of Chicago and affirms the importance of maintaining and, indeed, celebrating those values for the future.*

From its very founding, the University of Chicago has dedicated itself to the preservation and celebration of the freedom of expression as an essential element of the University's culture. In 1902, in his address marking the University's decennial, President William Rainey Harper declared that "the principle of complete freedom of speech on all subjects has from the beginning been regarded as fundamental in the University of Chicago" and that "this principle can neither now nor at any future time be called in question."

Thirty years later, a student organization invited William Z. Foster, the Communist Party's candidate for President, to lecture on campus. This triggered a storm of protest from critics both on and off campus. To those who condemned the University for allowing the event, President Robert M. Hutchins responded that "our students . . . should have freedom to discuss any problem that presents itself." He insisted that the "cure" for ideas we oppose "lies through open discussion rather than through inhibition." On a later occasion, Hutchins added that "free inquiry is indispensable to the good life, that universities exist for the sake of such inquiry, [and] that without it they cease to be universities."

In 1968, at another time of great turmoil in universities, President Edward H. Levi, in his inaugural address, celebrated "those virtues which from the beginning and until now have characterized our institution." Central to the values of the University of Chicago, Levi explained, is a profound commitment to "freedom of inquiry." This freedom, he proclaimed, "is our inheritance."

More recently, President Hanna Holborn Gray observed that "education should not be intended to make people comfortable, it is meant to make them think. Universities should be expected to provide the conditions within which hard thought, and therefore strong disagreement, independent judgment, and the questioning of stubborn assumptions, can flourish in an environment of the greatest freedom."

❖ ❖ ❖

The words of Harper, Hutchins, Levi, and Gray capture both the spirit and the promise of the

University of Chicago. Because the University is committed to free and open inquiry in all matters, it guarantees all members of the University community the broadest possible latitude to speak, write, listen, challenge, and learn. Except insofar as limitations on that freedom are necessary to the functioning of the University, the University of Chicago fully respects and supports the freedom of all members of the University community "to discuss any problem that presents itself."

Of course, the ideas of different members of the University community will often and quite naturally conflict. But it is not the proper role of the University to attempt to shield individuals from ideas and opinions they find unwelcome, disagreeable, or even deeply offensive. Although the University greatly values civility, and although all members of the University community share in the responsibility for maintaining a climate of mutual respect, concerns about civility and mutual respect can never be used as a justification for closing off discussion of ideas, however offensive or disagreeable those ideas may be to some members of our community.

The freedom to debate and discuss the merits of competing ideas does not, of course, mean that individuals may say whatever they wish, wherever they wish. The University may restrict expression that violates the law, that falsely defames a specific individual, that constitutes a genuine threat or harassment, that unjustifiably invades substantial privacy or confidentiality interests, or that is otherwise directly incompatible with the functioning of the University. In addition, the University may reasonably regulate the time, place, and manner of expression to ensure that it does not disrupt the ordinary activities of the University. But these are narrow exceptions to the general principle of freedom of expression, and it is vitally important that these exceptions never be used in a manner that is inconsistent with the University's commitment to a completely free and open discussion of ideas.

In a word, the University's fundamental commitment is to the principle that debate or deliberation may not be suppressed because the ideas put forth are thought by some or even by most members of the University community to be offensive, unwise, immoral, or wrong-headed. It is for the individual members of the University community, not for the University as an institution, to make those judgments for themselves, and to act on those judgments not by seeking to suppress speech, but by openly and vigorously contesting the ideas that they oppose. Indeed, fostering the ability of members of the University community to engage in such debate and deliberation in an effective and responsible manner is an essential part of the University's educational mission.

As a corollary to the University's commitment to protect and promote free expression, members of the University community must also act in conformity with the principle of free expression. Although members of the University community are free to criticize and contest the views expressed on campus, and to criticize and contest speakers who are invited to express their views on campus, they may not obstruct or otherwise interfere with the freedom of others to express views they reject or even loathe. To this end, the University has a solemn responsibility not only to promote a lively and fearless freedom of debate and deliberation, but also to protect that freedom when others attempt to restrict it.

As Robert M. Hutchins observed, without a vibrant commitment to free and open inquiry, a university ceases to be a university. The University of Chicago's long-standing commitment to this principle lies at the very core of our University's greatness. That is our inheritance, and it is our promise to the future.

Geoffrey R. Stone
*Edward H. Levi Distinguished Service Professor of Law, Chair*

Marianne Bertrand
*Chris P. Dialynas Distinguished Service Professor of Economics, Booth School of Business*

Angela Olinto
*Homer J. Livingston Professor, Department of Astronomy and Astrophysics, Enrico Fermi Institute, and the College*

Mark Siegler
*Lindy Bergman Distinguished Service Professor of Medicine and Surgery*

David A. Strauss
*Gerald Ratner Distinguished Service Professor of Law*

Kenneth W. Warren
*Fairfax M. Cone Distinguished Service Professor, Department of English and the College*

Amanda Woodward
*William S. Gray Professor, Department of Psychology and the College*

# Notes

1   Kelly later delivered his address at the William F. Buckley Jr. Program at Yale's second annual and aptly named "Disinvitation Dinner" in New York City.

2   Ayaan Hirsi Ali received two standing ovations when she later spoke at Yale, under the Buckley Program's auspices.

3   See, Valerie Strauss, "Scripps College Uninvites George Will Because of Column on Sexual Assault," *Washington Post*, October 8, 2014, https://www.washingtonpost.com/news/answer-sheet/wp/2014/10/08/scripps-college-uninvites-george-will-because-of-column-on-sexual-assault/.

4   See, Valerie Richardson, "Campus Paper Budget Yanked in Dust-Up over 'Black Lives Matter' Op-Ed," *Washington Times*, October 20, 2015, http://www.washingtontimes.com/news/2015/oct/20/wesleyan-students-slash-campus-newspaper-budget-af/.

5   Catherine Rampell, "Political Correctness Devours Yet Another College, Fighting over Mini-Sombreros," *Washington Post*, March 3, 2016, https://www.washingtonpost.com/opinions/party-culture/2016/03/03/fdb46cc4-e185-11e5-9c36-e1902f6b6571_story.html.

6   The exact resolution read: "Resolved: That society has a moral obligation to diagnose and treat tragic racial IQ inferiority." Alan Astrow et al., "Chauncey Call for Order Fails to Quell Disruption," *Yale Daily News*, April 16, 1974, at 1.

7   See, James H. Carter, "Political Union Withdraws Speaking Invitation to Alabama Segregationist Governor Wallace at Request of Kingman Provost [*sic*] Brewster," *Yale Daily News*, September 20, 1963, at 1.

8   In 1975, a student interviewed James Wood, the president of the Political Union in 1963. Wood claimed that the Political Union only postponed, rather than revoked, Wallace's invitation. Even if true, this would have been a distinction without a difference. See, Tom

Cavanagh, "George Wallace in '63: Disinvited or Postponed?" *Yale Daily News*, February 5, 1975, at 2. After the Political Union revoked or postponed the invitation, the World Community Association and the Yale Law Forum at the Yale Law School subsequently issued a new invitation to Wallace, despite Brewster's protests; Wallace declined to accept it. James H. Carter, "Mid-November Date Named," *Yale Daily News*, September 27, 1963, at 1; "Bulletin," *Yale Daily News*, October 1, 1963, at 1.

9    Interview with Henry "Sam" Chauncey Jr., former aide to Kingman Brewster, in New Haven, Connecticut, on February 14, 2013.

10   Scott Herhold, "Committee Readmits Suspended Students," *Yale Daily News*, November 11, 1969, at 1.

11   The Woodward Report does not include this incident in its history of free speech at Yale. The committee's minutes indicate that the members discussed the incident, though only once.

12   Woodward outlined the trajectory of his views on free expression in a speech entitled "Cycles of Academic Freedom," which can be found in his papers housed at Yale's Manuscripts and Archives.

13   See, Robert Dahl, *Who Governs? Democracy and Power in an American City* (New Haven: Yale University Press, 1961).

14   There is some evidence that Woodward softened his history to protect Kingman Brewster from excessive criticism. Those interested should see the author's article, Nathaniel Zelinsky, "Challenging the Unchallengeable (sort of)," *Yale Alumni Magazine*, January–February 2015, https://yalealumnimagazine.com/articles/4017/woodward-report.

15   In addition to Wellington, a second committee member, Lloyd Cutler, co-chaired the third section. Readers will know Cutler best as White House Counsel to Presidents Carter and Clinton. Cutler was likely on the committee to protect Brewster's interests. See Zelinsky, "Challenging the Unchallengeable (sort of)."

16   This booklet does not contain the dissent. Readers interested in an unedited version of the report can find one on Yale's website: http://yalecollege.yale.edu/deans-office/policies-reports/report-committee-freedom-expression-yale.

17 Richard Schumacher, "Anti-Gay Poster Sparks Free Speech Controversy," *Yale Daily News*, September 3, 1986, at 1.

18 Richard Schumacher, "Schmidt, Student Discuss Rehearing," *Yale Daily News*, September 4, 1986, at 1.

19 Richard Schumacher, "Wayne Dick Acquitted: May Decision Reversed after Lengthy Furor," *Yale Daily News*, October 22, 1986, at 1.

20 Peter Salovey, President, Yale University, Freshman Address, August 23, 2014, http://news.yale.edu/2014/08/22/professor-woodward-s-legacy-after-40-years-free-expression-yale.

21 "Important Updates on SAE and Buckley Investigations," *Yale News*, December 9, 2015, http://news.yale.edu/2015/12/09/important-updates-sae-and-buckley-investigations.

22 Eugene Volokh, "Administrator's Defending Student Free Speech Is Apparently Reason to Remove the Administrator, according to Some Yale Students," Volokh Conspiracy, *Washington Post*, November 7, 2015, https://www.washingtonpost.com/news/volokh-conspiracy/wp/2015/11/07/administrators-defending-student-free-speech-apparently-reason-for-dismissal-according-to-some-yale-students/.

23 Nicholas and Erika Christakis did resign in the spring of 2016, after the protests subsided. Around the same time, Yale changed the title "master" to "head of college." As part of the fall 2015 protests, students demanded the change, claiming that the word "master" traumatically evoked the history of slavery. Yale borrowed the title in the 1930s from British universities.

24 Peter Salovey, President, Yale University, Baccalaureate Address, May 22, 2014, http://news.yale.edu/2016/05/22/membership-community-speaking-listening-finding-common-ground-presidents-baccalaureate-ad.

THE WOODWARD REPORT

1 *Editor's note:* The Corporation is Yale's governing body of trustees, referred to as "fellows."

2 *Editor's note:* This reprinting of the report does not include the dissenter's statement. Those interested in the dissent may find it on

Yale's website: http://yalecollege.yale.edu/deans-office/policies-repo rts/report-committee-freedom-expression-yale.

3   *Editor's note:* Richard Herrnstein was a well-known Harvard psychologist and public intellectual who argued that intelligence was largely biologically, not environmentally, determined. He successfully spoke at Yale, despite the anticipation of disruption, in May 1972, shortly after the Westmoreland and Rogers incidents.

COMMENTARY

1   An earlier version of this commentary appeared in *Free to Teach, Free to Learn: Understanding and Maintaining Academic Freedom in Higher Education* (American Council of Trustees and Alumni, April 2013). The authors thank the American Council of Trustees and Alumni, and particularly Anne D. Neal, for soliciting the original commentary and for inviting us to consider these important issues.

2   For instance, excerpts from the Woodward Report also appear in the section on "free expression" in the Undergraduate Regulations of Yale College. See, *Yale College Undergraduate Regulations* 2015–2016 (revised August 20, 2015), at 47–49, http://yalecollege.yale. edu/sites/default/files/files/URs%202015-2016%281%29.pdf.

3   Judith Krauss and Peter Salovey, "Why Having Free Speech at Yale Matters," *Yale Daily News*, March 1, 2005, http://yaledailynews. com/blog/2005/03/01/why-having-free-speech-at-yale-matters. Salovey, now Yale's president, was then dean of Yale College. Judith Krauss was "master" of Silliman College.

4   *United States v. Schwimmer*, 279 U.S. 644, 654–55 (1929) (Holmes, J., dissenting).

5   U.S. Department of Justice, Civil Rights Division, and U.S. Department of Education, Office for Civil Rights, "Findings Letter" re. University of Montana (May 9, 2013), at 8, 9, https://www. justice.gov/sites/default/files/opa/legacy/2013/05/09/um-ltr-findings.pdf (emphasis supplied). These agencies announced this new standard at the conclusion of a federal investigation into the University of Montana's policies and practices regarding sexual

misconduct. The "findings letter" was accompanied by a "resolution agreement" between the federal government and the University of Montana, which the government described as "a blueprint for colleges and universities throughout the country." *Id.* at 1.

6   Conor Friedersdorf, "How Sexual-Harassment Policies Are Diminishing Academic Freedom," *Atlantic*, October 20, 2015, http://www.theatlantic.com/politics/archive/2015/10/sexual-harassment-academic-freedom/411427 (quoting speech by Nadine Strossen, professor of law at New York Law School).

7   OCR's definition omits two important elements of the usual definition of peer-on-peer harassment: that the conduct would be considered *objectively* offensive by a hypothetical "reasonable person" (not just *subjectively* offensive to *someone*), and that the conduct be "severe" and "pervasive" (not just an isolated incident). See, e.g., *Davis v. Monroe County Board of Education*, 526 U.S. 629, 633 (1999).

8   One prominent example was the treatment of Laura Kipnis, a liberal cultural critic and professor in the Department of Radio/TV/Film at Northwestern University, whose work focuses on "sexual politics" and related subjects. See her blog at http://laurakipnis.com/?page_id=2 (last visited June 1, 2016). Kipnis faced complaints filed with her university's Title IX coordinator based on an essay she wrote about growing "sexual paranoia" on college campuses, which she described as "to the detriment of those whose interests are supposedly being protected, namely students": Laura Kipnis, "Sexual Paranoia Strikes Academe," *Chronicle of Higher Education*, February 27, 2015, http://laurakipnis.com/wp-content/uploads/2010/08/Sexual-Paranoia-Strikes-Academe.pdf. In other words, it has become a chargeable offense to criticize the current Title IX regime, even from an avowedly feminist position. (Kipnis was ultimately cleared of wrongdoing.) See also Laura Kipnis, "My Title IX Inquisition," *Chronicle of Higher Education*, May 29, 2015, http://laurakipnis.com/wp-content/uploads/2010/08/My-Title-IX-Inquisition-The-Chronicle-Review-.pdf.

9   See, e.g., Greg Lukianoff, "The Department of Education, Yale, and

the New Threat to Free Speech on Campus," *Huffington Post*, August 15, 2011, http://www.huffingtonpost.com/greg-lukianoff/yale-the-department-of-ed_b_877467.html (discussing Yale's suspension of a fraternity, and the punishment of its individual members, because of its pledges' offensive chant); C. Ramsey Fahs, "In Historic Move, Harvard to Penalize Final Clubs, Greek Organizations," *Crimson*, May 6, 2016, http://www.thecrimson.com/article/2016/5/6/college-sanctions-clubs-greeklife (reporting Harvard University's decision to ban undergraduate members of single-sex social organizations from holding leadership positions or receiving endorsements for certain fellowships).

10  Courts have not yet resolved at what point the action of private universities becomes "state action" for constitutional purposes – i.e., subject to constitutional constraints – because it is effectively required by federal agencies.

11  See, e.g., "Yale Sexual Misconduct Policies and Related Definitions," Yale University (updated May 10, 2016), http://smr.yale.edu/sexual-misconduct-policies-and-definitions.

12  See, e.g., Haley Hudler, "Yale Students Demand Resignations from Faculty Members over Halloween Email," Foundation for Individual Rights in Education, November 6, 2015, https://www.thefire.org/yale-students-demand-resignations-from-faculty-members-over-halloween-email.

13  See, Catherine Rampell, "College Students Run Crying to Daddy Administrator," *Washington Post*, May 19, 2016, https://www.washingtonpost.com/opinions/college-students-run-crying-to-daddy-administrator/2016/05/19/61b53f54-1deb-11e6-9c81-4be1c14fb8c8_story.html (listing these and other examples from the University of Oregon).

14  For instance, a senior Yale administrator stated that the university was "'exploring a number of possibilities' for reporting incidents of sexual harassment and discrimination based on race, ethnicity, veteran status, sexual orientation and other protected categories." Maya Sweedler and Monica Wang, "Yale Considers Launching Harassment Site," *Yale Daily News*, April 22, 2016, http://yaledailynews.com/

blog/2016/04/22/yale-considers-launching-harassment-site. For coverage of anonymous reporting apps at other universities, see, e.g., Anna North, "A New Way to Report College Sexual Assault," *New York Times*, May 27, 2016, http://takingnote.blogs.nytimes.com/2016/05/27/a-new-way-to-report-college-sexual-assault.

15   For instance, the Supreme Court recently split 5–4 over the constitutionality of stopping a car based on an "anonymous" 911 report that the car had run the caller off the road. Justice Clarence Thomas, who wrote for the majority, called it a "close case," but ultimately concluded that such a stop was permissible. *Navarette v. California*, 134 S. Ct. 1683, 1692 (2014) (internal quotation marks omitted). Critical to the majority's reasoning was the possibility of tracing the call – and, thus, of punishing the caller, if necessary, for making a false report. See also *id.* at 1687 n.1 (noting that caller had "identified herself by name" when making her report); and note 16 below along with the accompanying text on page 64 above.

16   See, *Navarette v. California*, 134 S. Ct. 1683, 1689–90 (2014).

17   In addition, police, unlike administrators at private universities, face constitutional constraints when acting on anonymous tips.

18   Fortunately, some universities continue to defend free expression vigorously. Most prominently, in January 2015, the University of Chicago powerfully reaffirmed its longstanding commitment to "free and open discourse on campus" by issuing a document called – perhaps not coincidentally – the "Report of the Committee on Freedom of Expression." (The Woodward Report is formally titled "Report of the Committee on Freedom of Expression at Yale.") The Chicago report, reprinted in this booklet, illustrates how universities can continue to defend the enduring values expressed in the Woodward Report, even – indeed, especially – "in light of recent events nationwide that have tested institutional commitments to free and open discourse" (page 67 above).

First American edition published in 2016 by Encounter Books,
an activity of Encounter for Culture and Education, Inc.,
a nonprofit, tax exempt corporation.
Encounter Books website address: www.encounterbooks.com

Manufactured in the United States and printed on
acid-free paper. The paper used in this publication meets
the minimum requirements of ANSI/NISO z39.48–1992
(R 1997) (*Permanence of Paper*).

FIRST AMERICAN EDITION

LIBRARY OF CONGRESS CATALOGING-IN-PUBLICATION DATA

Names: Cabranes, Jose A., author. | Stith, Kate, author. | Zelinsky, Nathaniel A. G., author. | Yale University. Committee on Freedom of Expression at Yale. Report of the Committee on Freedom of Expression at Yale.

Title: Campus speech in crisis : what the Yale experience can teach America /

Jose A. Cabranes, Kate Stith, Nathaniel A. G. Zelinsky ; preface by George Will.

Description: New York : Encounter Books, 2016. | Includes reprint of the Report of the Committee on Freedom of Expression at Yale, published in 1975. | Description based on print version record and CIP data provided by publisher; resource not viewed.

Identifiers: LCCN 2016033045 (print) | LCCN 2016029297 (ebook) | ISBN 9781594039201 (Ebook) | ISBN 9781594039195 (paperback)

Subjects: LCSH: Academic freedom—United States. | Freedom of speech—United States. | Yale University—Students—Political activity—History—20th century. | BISAC: POLITICAL SCIENCE / Censorship. | EDUCATION / Higher. | POLITICAL SCIENCE / Political Freedom & Security / General.

Classification: LCC LC72.2 (print) | LCC LC72.2 .C33 2016 (ebook) | DDC
378.1/213–dc23

LC record available at https://lccn.loc.gov/2016033045

10 9 8 7 6 5 4 3 2 1

A NOTE ON THE TYPE

CAMPUS SPEECH IN CRISIS *has been set in Galliard, Matthew Carter's interpretation of the types of Robert Granjon. Originally created for photocomposition and later updated and reintroduced in digital form, Galliard has enjoyed continuous success among book designers since its first release in 1978. Strongly influenced by the chancery hands of the sixteenth century, Galliard – and particularly the italic face – possesses a lively calligraphic rhythm rarely seen in text types. Despite an august lineage that counts Granjon and Claude Garamond among its progenitors, Galliard retains a lightness and gaiety that readily recalls the dance after which it is named.*

DESIGN & COMPOSITION BY CARL W. SCARBROUGH